RUINOUS

KIANA LIN

For those who are lost in a cycle–
may we spiral upward.

CONTENTS

DESCEND

Disaster pulsing
Always beneath my skin,
Downfall breathing in my ears
Sweet promises.
The raging, biting, scraping
Inside my veins–
It is constant.

If I would loose
That choking, biting control–
If I only set free
The claws grasping, holding
My bones, my very being.
My emotions, my mind, my self
In check.

I could do it.
I could unleash it,
My forever, unrelenting darkness.
If I chose, I could be–
No.
However hidden, I am
Ruinous.

I was, am, livid, but you in your
Ignorance, you call me timid,
What do you know of cold rage?
What of calculation?
Darkly, quietly,
Anger comes now,
Without a
Single
Flash.

I've made my missteps,
Owned them.
But the unacknowledged
Mistakes of others–
Those are what cost me
The most.

You brandished your weapon with intention,
Challenging gaze meeting mine–
You said it was to be used on you.
But when wielding a knife,
Eyes remain fixed on the target.
And your gaze was locked upon my soul.

And I had a choice,
In those brief moments of eternity,
To either bend under the weight
Of your reckless manipulation
Or to rise and rise and rise
Above my own fears and expectations.

– It Was for Me.

Bright and wide-eyed for the beginning,
Unwakeable at the ending–
You hate that it's how I watch movies.
I hate that it's how you loved me.

I entwined our lives so completely,
When you picked apart your pieces,
Pulled on your threads–
It was all I could do not to unravel mine.

Somber, sullen, and sad–
A heart rejoicing at the thought,
The soul basking in the gloom.
How to know where the shadows begin,
To distinguish when I end?

I want to hear it.
Without once stopping to breathe–
Just say one real thing.

One word.
She held her breath
As long seconds passed,
Disappearing into something
Unspeakable.

Of excuses, I've heard enough:
It wasn't me . . .
I decided it would be better if–
I don't care.
I swear I never would–
If I'd known . . .
At this point, I'd rather that
You not pretend to–
Or even actually–be
Sorry.

It's sticky, weighted–
This feeling within
Welling up,
Dragging me down.
I am left with thoughts
Uncharitable.
Alone with my own self–
Graceless.

Inevitable.
It was all there,
The image of all the things–
The terrible things–
We could never forget
Happened.

How can the past be in the past
If history still has us in chains,
Still causes us to bleed anew,
Still echoes with voices
Withered and young?

Names carved into night.
Fresh sorrows now to behold
Within their stories.

The bizarre had arrived.
The doors were opened for our
Complete silence.
All to get a glance at holy nothing–
To see what grief looks like.

Everything was swaying–
Off–
As they bombarded you with the questions.
And every once in a while
Someone tried to reach out, to tell you:
I know.
But it can't happen, can it?
How could they?
Just like the first time,
They have more questions.
And you can never give the answers.

What's your question?
Deep in thought–
A dead, killed thought.
She waited,
But nothing else came.

-Never Mind.

A mind ill-made for stillness,
A form so devoid of urgency–
Yet they ask why she lives
Always within her head.

Heavy, sluggish eyes,
Body too solid to lift,
Weighted, muted emotions.
If only my thoughts
Were as grounded,
Were not racing
At speeds that leave me–
My very being,
To drown.
Shackled by the burdens
Of those abandoned ideas
From a mind
That is continuously
Leaving my body behind,
To wallow in these sheets.

The responsibility–of being the center,
Of the attention.
It transformed, changing the feelings,
Again and again,
Until she screamed in her head.
In desperation, pleading for help,
Hoping that with so many eyes,
Someone might somehow see.

Three seconds to explain,
But how to say what you don't know.
You think this is love.
Their rock-throwing looked
Like the attention you were used to,
Like the affection of the one
Whose words you once craved.
But the three moments passed,
And it's too late to make them understand.

I know what they think,
The words they whisper into
Ears that are not mine.

She only smiled.
Twilight creeping across the sky–
Mysterious.
She smiled, breaking.

It's worse–
More terrible than mere disrespect.
Eviscerating
In the same way as intentional
Disregard.
The painful, shattering feeling of being
Unknowingly
Unknown.

Can you imagine a
Death that takes a taste
Without consuming?
An internal chipping away
Of something unseen,
Buried deep within.
It is a slow crumble
As the soul is leaking
Down the rough exterior.
A constant drip,
A slow trickle–
The rivulet of blood that erodes
Without becoming the river
That carries away the stone.

I'm hiding inside, somewhere.
It's the only thing I can do
To prove I can find
Just one normal day.
A hoax,
A form of reassurance–
As if the world can be okay again.

A pretty voice
That sounded in her skull.
The voice,
Real or a dream?
But all the same,
Every word spelled it out–
The end.

It never could fly on it's own,
Not alive and tethered as it was.
Roots hold it upright–yes,
And also batten it down.
But dead, loosed?
Well, freedom comes
In so many forms.

I change, but in death
I am made immutable.
"Always" has a price.

All the same.
We'll make the change later,
Later.
A quiet sigh, a go-around–
The only one to ever say no.
She put some thought into it.
Maybe, we can talk.
Talk about me,
Like I'm not here.
The surprise was surreal.
It hadn't really hit,
Until then.

How quickly the light disappeared.
The air around, muted–
Beautiful and fallen.
Deeper it darkened,
Losing, with every second,
Any sign,
As if it never existed.

If she had only known,
And perhaps she didn't do this–
Not on purpose–
But she didn't stop it.
She was too busy to notice
What was slipping away,
Was about to close.

She couldn't remember.
She was comatose.
A few drips of thought at a time–
Everything just to keep her alive,
Surviving.
She talks in her sleep.
She might wake up and be okay.
It's impossible to understand,
But it all has to end to continue.
Over and over.
Born to die.
A maddening itch inside
That won't go away.

As if things
Skipped a beat,
But didn't slow.
I am unsettled,
Am left unsure.

Distraction
Distance between what you pursue and what you
Desire.
Dissonance within yourself, made outward.
Damned,
Detained by the accumulation of momentary
Derailments.
Done in by all the things that never made it beyond
Daydreams.

What, then, is faith?
Is it merely the desire to believe?
Or, perhaps, it is action
Despite all the reasons to doubt?
Whichever it may be,
Surely it is not this sinking feeling.

Silent.
She didn't feel.
She had disappeared,
Nowhere to be seen.
She was fabricated–
Artificial.
Eyes glued to the hurt,
Until all she could sense,
All she could think:
Maybe something's broken.
Too far gone.
Maybe it won't come back.

Something once so deep, so true–
I could see them all as you spoke,
Imagined them filling with thoughts.
But that was a shallow, remembered well.
A treacherous and dried up place
Now passed in silence,
Devoid and bleak.

All was order, quiet.

She didn't know how much longer she could last.

Too quiet,

Thoughts darting around, familiar.

Why would she make that up?

She put too much stock in disguise.

She couldn't stay silent another second.

Raising the volume,

Grasping for the right words,

The swirling in her mind

About who she really was.

How wonderful life is,
When you don't live
In a world of circles.
I stopped moving,
Just to see.
And I watched as we
Descended into the black
Without even trying.

Follow her back to the morning.
Crawl out from under
The dead,
The shadowed.
She showed us more than just
Wandering glimpses of light–
Never known in full.
It seemed so ordinary
To be left in the dark.
At least to us.

The cliff was always there,
Waiting.
You stepped up,
Bent down,
Reached out–
Cascading over and pulling down
Everyone
Who had gathered behind,
Waiting for your fear
To finally give way.
They could have stopped it–
You wished they did!
But instead,
They fell with you,
Just so you wouldn't be
Alone.

The hint of a smile,
Vanishing.
Wiped fresh at your considering.
Maybe we shouldn't.

Though she didn't know what it meant,
Standing so close,
Murmuring in hushed tones.
When all finally ended,
She was left with it–
An intense feeling of nothing but
Arms empty, waiting.

I tried to grasp tighter,
Hold on and complete the picture.
But, there they were–still,
Left behind.

Are you owed consistency?
Has life ever been promised
Without compromise?
Why do you expect
To carry out your days
In pleasant expectation?
The random,
The inexplicable–
That is the guarantee
Of existence.

Too focused on a word,
Couldn't sleep–ready to do anything
To get my mind off of it.
Absently, a loose thought of you,
Of the odd connection.
For a word, "maybe" is as good
As any other.

Intentions, tar black,
Words, white as pearls.
Left there, again–
Cut off,
Lifeless,
Reforming.
And then, once more,
Back with heart in hand.

Through a glass filled with darkness,
I have seen you as you seem.
Yet, when this world has sunk
Through the glaring sun–
The throne finally taken for my own–
Only then, will I fully know your spirit.
But,
Not till then.
Not till then.
Not till then.

The itch to go,
To burst forth in all her glory,
Spinning without saying anything.
An intense curiosity to breathe–
Her darkness laced with memories.

Watch as it gleams,
Glitters with forbidden knowledge,
The secrets of fate winking,
Urging you on.
As if it had to be.

A thought mostly remembered,
Yet, I'm still searching for words.
Perhaps what will come
Is better than what is living now,
And–when it falls–
A better place will be found
Rising up.

You left me for dead,
Cold and limp.
So I breathe sharp air,
Expand my own aching lungs.
I pour molten steel
Upon my own spine,
Straightening, stiffening bone.
I raise my own self
From the mediocre, the decay,
Into new strength and life.

You put me
Between a rock and a hard place,
And I have made my home
In your crevices and cracks.
Watch as I take root–
And thrive as you crumble.

Hear my words
For what they are,
Without dismissing my voice
Because the tones
Are not what *you* would
Desire them to be.

I was born in the season
Where things go to die.
I was raised by their fall,
Brought alive by their bleaching rot.
My edges were hardened by
The sharp chill of autumn's air.
Why, then, do you wonder
How I became a force of nature?

A wolf cannot exist
In suspension.
She is trouble,
Alive and disconcerting.
It was impossible
For her to live inside–
Nothing but a crazy dream
To think
She could be contained
In lieu of running
Through the unruly open.

It was only everything–
Becoming undone–
Her eyes unmaking
All that they touched.
She'd rolled
Right up against the night,
Awake.
Then whispered, just to know
Something had awaited
Her arrival in the dark.
Everything in the night rejoiced,
Joined her and echoed back:
I'm awake.

CLIMB

Still nothing–
No light, no sound.
The anticipation passed,
Her chest felt numb.
Then,
In a sudden burst of life,
It started:
Unfurling.

Silence followed
Right behind the spiraling cold.
Stay–for once.
Speak, please!
Nothing, something?
Trying to deny,
Too terrified to see.
Whispers in a daze–
The trickle of understanding,
The wait for resolution,
The end of the usual.
All of it necessary to take
The very first step of hope.

She didn't get the rules yet,
But plenty of people told her what it's like.
She took a deep breath to gain strength.
She was always the one–
The one with all the experience and knowledge,
The willpower to push.
But then, someone came alongside her,
Showed her:
I've been here and I've seen it too–
The final, calm nothing.
She could now let go.

I feel your cold tears,
And yet they are drying fast–
Shared breaths evening.

The shadows ran long in her mind.
Without meaning to–
Or even realizing–
They found their path.
The way had been right,
The night already at an end.

More and more elaborate,
You give a frustrated sigh.
For the first time,
Why don't you quit
Defiantly burying everything?

It carried her further than she expected,
But then,
Stopped so abruptly.
She had almost gone over without realizing.
It had led her right up to
The edge,
The abyss,
The shadow.
She came to and pulled away,
Despite her body still pulling her forward,
Her mind brought her back to herself,
To safety.

This fault in blood,
I want it to be the end
Of your hold on me.
The attachment, once open,
Finally closed.

Crouched, wedged,
Stilted by the thought.
Is it curiosity or dread?
Either way,
The only choice left–
Move.

How do you know?
Because . . .
She trailed off.
Through the changing–
All night, days later–
After what we went through,
I think
We've survived.

What changed?
It all seemed comfortable
At the time.
Things would be okay–
I was still awake.
But then I thought about it,
Felt the walls when I stretched.
Wherever this was coming from,
This thing from outside
Of myself–
I wanted it.

The darkness of early morning
Melted away–
The whisper before
The wake up.

New life in cold darkness,
Fresh air and solid ground and hoping eyes.
The workings of an ancient echo.
The ascended senses alone and waiting–
Thought, the only thing.
Flooded with facts and images,
Memories and details.
The world, the moon:
Turning on.

Concentrate beyond what you hear now.
Welling out from grief,
The words are sharp.
A moment before the tears start,
Take heart in the familiar.
Memories, emotions,
Things found missing from your life–
The very things needed.

Our eyelids flutter
As we think of a thousand things.
Perhaps we just need to sleep,
To be outside, in the thicker woods,
To sit and rest.
Until we know.

A dangerous mindset–
Or so they say.
Honestly, it could've been worse.

It is taken as self-deprecating,
Because that's what they can comprehend.
Still, it could've been worse.

The hope, strength, and realism,
The unlimited perspective–discarded.
But . . . It could've been worse.

Words of the survivors,
A battered phrase that leads to the fight:
Even so, it could be worse.

It is a continuous
Inundation
Of small things
That shatter a person.
So, of course, it is a
Gentle repetition
Of little gestures
That heal them.

Eyes that blink slowly,
Often hide a mind brimming–
Possibility.

Push,
If you must.
Wake up and lean out.
And then come back,
As you will.

Trying to get somewhere,
Only,
I wonder where?
Tickling the mind to life,
Feeling the soft,
The slow,
The something–
Always a feeling
Of wanting, needing, more.
Perhaps just a little bit
Further?

Loyalty so freely given,
But trust is hard to come by.
The opposites tearing,
The commonalities stretching.
Even so,
It remains unbroken, somehow.
Yet what should be simple
Gets muddled and confused
The reconciliation, unbearable.
And still.

My heart knows what to do,
But my head is snarled.
In my mind is an idea,
Yet my chest is an ocean.
As soon as the bridge is crossed,
I've already forgotten my purpose.
The opposing sides switch,
Taking up one another's causes.
My head knows what to do,
But my heart is tangled.
In my chest is an idea,
But my mind is an ocean.

Am I a thinker of deep thoughts?
An explorer,
Excavating long-buried emotions?
Or am I simply making mountains
Of momentary molehills?

Why even pretend,
Why entertain the hope of fairness?
Far better to expect nothing
And keep giving and giving–just because.
The rewards are the same,
There are fewer disappointments,
And best yet: Peace of mind.

Screaming into the void,
They say.
Perhaps–no, definitely,
I am.
But if it works, then–
Why not?

The world was frozen in place.
She was standing,
Once again,
But she looked worse:
Clothes ripped,
Covered in cuts and bruises,
As good as dead–
But still alive.
At least, a little.

One thing at a time,
Spilling onto the sizable pile.
Nothing but to memorize
These fleeting moments–
Just hold on to the hope
That it'll work
Eventually.

Without a moment to think,
Taking turn after turn,
She never paused.
Every inch hurt–
Inside and out–
But her heart didn't quit
Pumping.

Death is a looming presence.
A fear that follows and intrudes–
Even from the beginning.
A haunting eventuality
For which we prepare,
And dwell
And commiserate
And grieve–
Yet, for all that,
It only ends us once.
How much more are the opportunities
For which we live?
How many of the days of our lives
Do we sacrifice to death?
If you only die once,
How many times will you truly be alive?

Heart ready,
With breath
Just to get around
The next corner–
Time and again.

Dead, deep down–
All the important things had been swept over.
Go, they said, *stay out there.*
Try to explore the walls,
Look to the sky–
What a way to wake up!
She still felt it, though:
The cold permeating even their sunshine,
Those walls they wanted her to look past.
And they were so afraid of her natural power.
The only thing–to bring her down.
Knock the feeling, they said.
For good this time.

Hoping for the strength
To deal with what comes next.
I'd tried to control it somehow,
A thought changing the threat–
To make sure it never happens.
Again.
A heavy price for mere luck,
For certain uncertainty.
Thrown in thought,
I believe I'm not that person anymore.
Then again,
Being mostly alone sometimes sounds
Beautiful.

Nothing but embers
The only question that's left:
Burn higher or out?

SLIDE

Shouldn't I be past this?
The ebb and flow of these thoughts,
The force and drain of these emotions,
The inevitability of this cycle,
Where I circle back to this point.
When all I can ask, back at the start is:
Shouldn't I be past this?

There is a war behind my eyes,
Those windows you peer within
And declare vacant.
It's just that the shades are drawn,
A convincing setting superimposed
To hide the turmoil and deafening noise
Inside.

The opposing camps, forever divided,
Make no attempts to quiet
Their chaotic din, the clashes,
The war cries, the clanging thoughts.
There will be no resolution,
Not through peace nor understanding,
No.

Instead, there will be only bloodshed
In trickling streams of tears
That manage to escape the glassy fixtures.
The only end to the raging
Is when one side utterly decimates the other.
There can be no co-existence
Ever.

And just when the dust settles,
The droplets stoppered and dried,
The impossible happens.
The dead are raised
And come back with a vengeance.
So the battles go on and on
Forever.

You were like gravity:
I watched as everyone seemed
Caught up by your pull.
You thought my attention was inevitable,
You were thrown by my resistance.
Greater beings than I
Had been enslaved to your whims,
But you miscalculated.
You thought me so grounded as to be
Grateful for your time.
Yet I longed to fly,
To float–
To be free of your inconvenient,
Tethering opinions–
That which was meant to drag me back
Away from the stars,
From weightless bliss.

For someone
So longing for flight and freedom,
I seem to bind,
To chain,
To cement myself–
With everything on hand–
To everything in sight.

She didn't need to look
To know it would all end.
But she slipped closer–
She just kept moving, knowing:
There is darkness ahead,
Her plunging end below.

Tension.
Distrust feels like constriction.
Clenched teeth,
Hollow stomach,
Inability to breathe.
Would that I could let this go,
But my mind and fists are vises.

If you try to force feed me certainty,
I will disregard you completely.
If you wish for my attention,
Speak plainly,
Give me substance
And sustenance.
Give me the ugly truths as a meal.
For every course, serve up the harsh realities,
And for desert, I will accept a bite
Of your pretty hopes.

Haunted with: *Just maybe.*
A faint memory tried to escape
Within her mind.
Somewhere,
Something to think about . . .
Kept coming back,
No matter how hard she tried
To kill it.

You scream and wail:
It is the end of everything,
In one breath.
With the very next,
You whisper: *It's not over.*
Which "you" do I believe?

We balance, together, on the rim–
If I could only jump it.
It's possible, you say.
It's not magic, just some kind of mirage.
Even so, with as much as we know,
We still–without saying a word–
Reluctantly followed one another away.

A bridge to nowhere,
The ending obscured,
Unsupported,
Crumbling.
All because you won't give me
Even just the illusion of
A soft place to land.

The desire for what I can't have–
Let me forget and start sleeping.
Give me a rest, a reprieve,
While you make me wait.

Imagine it!
But she realized more.
How they must be like this,
At least for now.

Better things—this I promise.
My heart sank.
As if things hadn't been enough already.
I can't forget before,
Through the changing times.
Pause—
Look at each person from the past.
One last thing to do:
To say whatever you have to say
To be free.

He left without a word.
To be alone
Again.
Her mind wandered back
Every time she blinked.
She felt it in her bones–
One thing, even now.

Enough to fill the depths of the ocean,
More than the reaches of galaxies,
So much left unspoken behind the words:
There's nothing left to say.

In the circling of arms
It is hateful choice
And fear
And strange alarms.
Alone, my heart can rest.

Feeling sicker by the second,
With eyes closed, breathing made awkward,
Thinking and dreading what to say.
Then, after a long moment,
The door for understanding creaked open.
She thought to say sorry–
Thought of so many words–
But, before a single one was voiced,
The door slammed shut.
Hearts, now alone in echoing rooms.

Things to think about:
The secluded place where
Wonder,
Quiet,
And stillness
Lay.
The perfect place,
If it weren't torn apart.
Some things were just too perfect
To exist for long.

The cool caress of tears
Soothing the emotions left bruised
By words that hit too hard.

Eyes that finally shut.
A piercing cry with
That different voice, and
That same tear trickling down
A different face.

Sleep–rest!–so you can understand.
Then wake up to it–
No longer a mystery.
All we know
Is still enough to realize:
The old life was no better
Than what we have now.

I quit bothering
A long time ago.
Those words burning holes
In her mind,
In the walls,
In a breath.
There's nothing left,
Nothing to feed that flame
Anymore.

Cracked roots dug deep
As towering trees filled the sky.
Time breathed sweet feelings
That flared with the contact
Of the air, winds
Which turned so quickly.

The drops
That cause you to flourish,
Are the tide that–to me–
Is death.

She felt always, completely.
In order to drown out her head
They say, *Wait it out.*
Wishing she were miles away,
Finally breaking, finally screaming–
Yet no one seemed to hear,
To notice.
She never felt seen,
But always unbearably present.

Laughter.
The onslaught of words
Gilded with anger–
Enough to haunt forever.
Eyes on fire,
But not sure what to do next.
So, without saying a word,
She pushed past.

A shred of self-control prevented the tears.
She crawled to the edge,
Once more,
She crawled into whatever lay
Far,
Far
Below.
Things she'd never known
Existed.

A desire that is in my bones,
The creeping vine in my mind,
The unbreakable thread binding my soul:
A burning belief that I can always–
Always–
Put things back together.
This innate staple has almost
Always
Brought me to the brink
Of being undone.

There is beauty in the world,
But what I seek to remember,
What needs recollection,
Is not the brightness.
What is worth reflection are the real times.
The thick of the darkness,
The raw and the truth and the horror–
Our very mortality.

Too fascinated to see that I left them
Too shaken.
Hard to believe that their bones rattled,
Heads spinning.
It seemed impossible that there was still
More unknown.

Overcome with curiosity,
She'd yet to speak.
The questions formed–
Rose up–
And collapsed back to the ground.

In my mind is eloquence.
The thoughts travel to my chest,
Swirl within my lungs,
Mingling with the air I breathe
To become words.
They hold in my throat
While I wait for the opportune time,
The chance to release the beauty
Pent up in my darkness.
And when the moment arises,
Out of my mouth
Comes stilted, tangling nonsense.

– Of Course.

Write, they say, *about anything.*
But, you think, *there's still more to talk about–*
Time and words not spent
On scribbling new ways to ask:
Why?

A smile,
Shabbily built,
Yet supporting all the weight
Of her hopes and joys–
Because needs must.

Those things she had said,
Something about her that no one else knew.
She would keep it that way.
Nothing crazy,
Acting like things were alright,
Just thinking, not complaining–
It was the only thing she could do,
The closest thing to normal.
And they couldn't care less.
She paused, one more try.
A deep breath and then all that was left:
Run.

Everything is refashioning.
She tried to fight it,
To stay rigid, but,
Everything moves–
Forward to the last.

This changing world
Is lost in a brighter,
Brighter world.
The over-exposure
Making everything seem
Less tangible,
Less real,
Less.

Mourn the deaths
Of all the concepts,
The ideas that came and went,
The could-have-been's
That were sacrificed
By those who dismissed
The quiet beginnings,
The initial sparks–
Grieve the brilliance
That never made it
Past a feeling.

It is called dual nature,
And we are taught to fear it.
Told that those
Who suffer from it are unstable.
Yet I feel it.
Deep inside my bones,
Hiding in my mind,
Tainting my blood.
Am I more human
For having both light and dark inside me,
Or does having more
Somehow,
Make me less?

Before the realization, the tears,
More than twenty years–rewritten
In just one thought, an instant.
First the body reacts,
Knows before the brain,
And then the mind
Catches up
And still,
Tears.

It's a kind of fading–
I try to talk about it.
But there is something choking me,
Something that feels like remembering.
You were with me,
You felt the words,
The memories.
I can only hope–
If the world is the way I saw it,
If you knew me before–
Can't you tell me
If I'm still me?

I fall to sleep like this:
Quietly,
With memories that are small,
But everything.
Real,
Solid,
Essential,
And maddening.
But, I swear–
This is the last time.

Open your being to discovery,
For anything, anything at all.
Nothing may happen that first night.
An unshuttered mind a far cry
From keeping secrets.
Slowly carefully,
Feel the blankness.
What does it all mean,
Does it feel familiar?
Know it.
The desire to be free,
To feel the thoughts wandering
Inside that brain of yours.
Seek it out,
The darkness in your mind.
From now on, reside there–
Free to sleep at last.

Glass flowers–the epitome of
Beauty.
Don't you find it intriguing,
Fascinating?
The concept of taking something
Fragile,
Turning it into something endless,
Immortal.
For me, it is the process of arresting something
Transient,
A moment in time that is perpetually
Dying,
Yet, somehow, it will never quite be
Dead.

Have you ever felt
The feathered touch of
Scores of legs,
Miniscule and constant,
Brushing against your skin?
Do you know the thrill and the fear
Induced by the knowledge
That those tickles
Could so easily be the precursor
To burning, blinding pain–
That any of those limbs
Could turn out to be
The two stingers
That strike to bring you down?
No? Perhaps, instead,
You are familiar with the terrible,
Uncertain balance that is

- Hope.

We're messed up,
She said,
And scared–
So trust me.

He began to ask *how,*
When she thought aloud.
If you tried,
I bet you could.

Hearing the words,
Everything clicked.
I know.
I'm ready.
The only thing left
Was courage
And
Every
Millisecond
Of
Waiting.

The home she'd made for herself,
The shelter constructed from her old fear–
Her heart reminded her that it wasn't real,
Reminded her that she still
Dreamt.
But she couldn't stop thinking,
Even though she felt the moment that
The before
Became
The after.
Even though she felt herself waking.

Only a flash.

A relentless jumble–as if from a nightmare.

Like a burst through the blood,

And–finally–sucking in deep breaths:

She took that first look

At what she had become.

Nature takes its course,
And it doesn't last.
Still, she opens her eyes,
Quietly looking to smolder,
Become breathing embers,
To burn to the end.

In time, my thoughts turned
To love and hate
And died under all the civilization.
This interpretation,
This imitation of life
That molded the social order I knew,
The construct I want buried.

A promise–
And I felt it burn.
Hope just beyond the window,
Glass panes made up of that vow
Which I whispered to no one.

Perish all I've sought
And hoped
Or known–
I have stayed my heart
And heaven.
I am still my own.
Storms will rage,
Even now clouds gather–
All for me.

A howling phenomenon,
My outburst in the rain.
Still in a state of shock,
And–while I don't really mind–
I draw the line here.

Her head would never be domesticated.
His idea of spirit,
Something ridiculously embellished:
With gold and embroidery,
Red plush and frill.
He grabbed hold.
At the same time,
She stood ready–
Shifting and restless–
Insatiable.

She is proud, standing tall still,
Despite the scars from long exposure
To harsh and unforgiving elements.
She has known better days,
Lived in the night mists
Amongst the crumbling ghosts of yesterdays.
And–smoke rising from within–
She has wrapped herself in crackling flames.
She has stared into nothing but sorrows,
And now, there is strength in her,
A power that burns.

The shadows are draped becomingly,
Lovely to her person.
Not because she belongs in darkness,
But because she is mystery,
Best glimpsed by a shard of light
And otherwise left to her secrets.

ASCEND

Escape–
An impossible solution.
This is my life,
She thought.
Living surrounded by the familiar depths,
No memory of life before the dark.
Then, a burst of warmth–
So needed.
She didn't realize how much she'd forgotten
Until it started.

She could imagine it so clearly,
The world outside this box.
Glancing up at the glass that became granite,
The walls that served as the windows.
The thought made her wonder,
The wondering became a discovery–
The realization
That she was already through,
Already out.

A glimpse of light
Above fear.
I spent so long below,
In darkness,
The wave of foreign shadows.
And then,
To see the fright melted away,
Overcome.

Love, give me indifference
By the pale light of dawn.
That dream–
The reality had been the dream,
And it once again calls,
Come.

Something I don't believe in
Cut like a knife through the lie.
I can't fathom that the answer was
Simply
Feeling.

It's cold outside,
Yet all I feel is warmth.
The sky is dark,
But I just see the lights.
Leaves tremble to their deaths,
And I have never been so alive.

Waking up, heart slowing–
Mind at peace.
It was different, so different,
An experience I haven't had in a while.
Now, finally, alert and seen.
Remember me?

It seemed impossible to get closer,
Always stumbling backward again.
But their hands were still clasped,
As she tugged.
Muscles flexed as he pulled
Until finally,
Inch by inch,
Against the struggling,
They moved, up and away.
Slowly, they calmed,
Breaths evening,
Everything held firm–
The ordeal truly ended.

You asked
If I was sure,
And I told you
I was certain.
You asked:
What is the difference?
And I told you,
It's more than a thought
In your mind.
It is knowing
In your bones.

He whispered meaning:
We've all come out
Of that dark truth,
But the exit is still
Further down the road.

It defied any sense,
But then
It took shape with every step away.
Somehow,
It just seemed like a moment
For a new direction.

I saw what could possibly be.
And I can't remember why, she said,
But don't let me forget what I've seen.
It was a connection,
So needed, so misunderstood.
He offered up his hand,
Holding onto hers for a long time.
That was it.
This is all I want.

I can love because
I can trust that
My soul is here,
From day to day–
Here to stay.

Was that really just yesterday?
How it could've been–
Isn't this how it's always been?
The question, the choice, that,
Inexplicably,
Made time settle in this place.

Tomorrow,
You'll be there–
The only thing in the world–
Needed.

A thought sprang out–
They do always come at night–
One little spark of hope.
Almost in a daze, she realized:
Haven't you more than the everyday?

Trying to visualize the future,
Hoping we come back–
One day–
To a place we can rest.

Nothing wasted,
Everything gained.
If only you view
These troubles–
Those times–
As something to unmake you,
To create you.
A you that can be
Better for it.

Truth is breath.
Breathe slowly,
Repeat often.
Honesty becomes you.

It's meant to be brief–
A simple spark.
A single puff and death comes.
It wavers, contemplates.
Then, even so, stands strong.

Focus.
Deep, expanding–
In and out.
Stillness of mind.
Strength of soul,
Long breaths–
Out and in.
Clarity.

Let it stay with you,
In memory, at least.
Let it rest with you,
Finding safe harbor
Until it can take root,
Can grow beyond your sheltered mind–
Can become action.

As we compare
Day to day,
Week to week,
We haven't yet figured out
What we're looking for,
But we can't give up.
We can't give up
Going for real.
No more thinking about
Ready or not.
Let's just run
One step at a time.

A minute passed,
Several more.
Change revolves around
Leaning forward, moving on,
And–frozen for just a moment–
Making the tough decisions.
Even if it means bouncing backward
So you can remain undamaged,
Before leaning in
Once again.

Whatever has come before,
The worst is yet to arrive.
For all my fortitude,
I am not prepared–
Nor will I ever be.
Even so,
You may send it my way.

Peace is not inherently human,
Despite our best attempts at the portrayal.
No.
What is at the base of our nature
Is the thrill of the fight.
So, I say, to battle.
Peace is earned through the struggle,
Achieved at the price of being burned.
If you want honest light,
Gaze into the flames of change.

The stuff of dreams cannot be made real,
That darkness must stay in shadow,
Yet I tried to bring it in,
Tried to make it alright.
Instead I hurt you,
An innocent,
For my own
Want of
Light.

-Forgive Me

Drooping, all the way to the ground,
Wrapped entirely in the darkness.
But,
Still attached up there–
Somewhere–
It held.
The mind so concentrated on
The brightness that could be.

The noises grew louder.
The roar,
The rolling,
The cranking.
She told herself
Quit waiting for the end
And listen–
Buh-bum.
Buh-bum.
Still alive.

Take hold of it.
The flushed face,
The eyes flamed with risk,
Just trying to live–
Own it.

Push, test the right
To climb,
To clamber up
Over and over,
Little by little.
Revel in the effort
Of every breath.

Too tired to fight,
Not ready to give it up,
Still no time to quit.

ABOUT THE AUTHOR

Ruinous is Kiana Lin's fourth full-length work, and she is–of course–still writing! To follow along on her journey and learn more, visit her website:

www.creativeinklin.com

Ever since she was a child, Kiana Lin has had a love of words. From her first made up phrase (to fit her stubborn idea) to learning to read (out of a spiteful need for independence), she took in every bit of wordplay and storytelling craft that she could. Then, one summer, a creative writing assignment led to a late brainstorming session in her aunt and uncle's kitchen. That one night sparked the desire to create something she would enjoy reading for herself.

And then she never stopped.

CPSIA information can be obtained
at www.ICGtesting.com
Printed in the USA
BVHW081726100522
636629BV00008B/954

9 781736 325568